CREATIVE CRAFTS

CREATIVE CRAFTS

MOIRA BUTTERFIELD

CHARTWELL
BOOKS, INC.

A QUARTO BOOK

Published by
Chartwell Books
A Division of Book Sales, Inc.
PO Box 7100
Edison, New Jersey 08818-7100

This edition produced for sale in the U.S.A., its
territories, and dependencies only.

ISBN 0-7858-0463-3

This book was designed and produced by
Quarto Children's Books Ltd
The Fitzpatrick Building
188-192 York Way
London N7 9QP

Editors Simon Beecroft and Samantha Hilton
Designer Michael Leaman
Photographer Paul Forester
Indexer Hilary Bird

Creative Director Louise Jervis
Senior Art Editor Nigel Bradley

The publishers would like to thank Dawn Apperley and Juliet Taylor for their artistic input.

Typeset by Michael Leaman Design Partnership
Manufactured by Regent Publishing Services Ltd, Hong Kong
Printed by C & C (Offset) Ltd, Hong Kong

Contents

Getting started

I N THIS BOOK THERE ARE LOTS OF DIFFERENT crafts for you to try. Each section shows projects which are simple enough for beginners, and there are lots of suggestions for other ideas to experiment with. The projects have all been designed so that you can get good results quickly and cheaply.

▲ *A papier mache bowl makes a great gift for a special someone!*

SUCCESSFUL CRAFTS

Before you choose which craft idea to make, think about who it is for and how it will be used.

If you are making something as a present for someone, think about the kind of taste they have: for instance, what style of clothes they wear and what ornaments they have in their home. If you follow their taste when you make something for them, your present is more likely to be a success.

If you are making something for yourself, use your favorite colors. You could even work your name or references to your hobbies into the design.

If you are making something to display in a particular room, think what color the room is, and then match or contrast the colors of the craft item you intend to make. You could adapt the design according to the activity in a particular room; for instance, you could use images of different foods for a kitchen object, and images of fish, boats, and mermaids for a bathroom object.

▲ *This snake is made by a method of fabric painting known as batik.*

needle

cotton reels

CRAFT KIT

It's a good idea to start gathering together a basic craft kit which will be useful whichever project you try. You will need to buy some of the items, but you can collect the others over time.

• Buy a pencil, water-washable glue, sticky tape, scissors, water-washable paints, a selection of paintbrushes, and a set of crayons. A sketchpad would be useful, too.
• For some of the crafts in this book you also need a small sewing kit, including pins, a needle, and some thread.

• Collect scrap paper and card, clean empty plastic pots and cartons, scrap fabric, wool, and catalogues.
• To store your craft kit, get a large empty cardboard box (you could find one in a supermarket). Decorate the box with paint or cut-out paper shapes.
• Buy a few special items for some crafts, such as fabric paints or cold-water dye.
• Before you start a craft, make sure you read the instructions for the product you buy.

CHOOSING A CRAFT

▲ *Designing your own wrapping paper makes a present really special.*

When you choose a craft to try, bear in mind how much time you have and how much money you want to spend to get the equipment and materials you need. For instance, if you want to complete a craft in a few hours, don't choose papier mache, which takes a few days to complete. If you don't want to buy any extra materials, try a craft such as collage, using items you already have around the house.

Don't worry if you don't get the exact results shown in the book. Use the photographs of objects as guides to help you create your own original pieces.

Poster paints and paintbrush

Pins

Scissors

Craft planning

Before you start a craft it is important to plan your work carefully. Make rough sketches and color them in with crayons or felt-tip pens, so you have some idea of what the finished design will be.

Colored paper

DESIGN RESEARCH

You may find that there is something special that you want to draw or paint. For instance, you may want to make a design in the shape of an animal. In that case, go to the library and find a book that shows you the shape and colors you need. You could also put real objects in front of you, such as leaves and flowers, and copy what you see.

Many of the crafts in this book are traditional. Once you get interested in a particular method, go to the library and find books on craft techniques and design in history. Look out for inspiration in museums and art galleries, too.

DESIGNING IDEAS

Gather together pencils, crayons, an eraser, a ruler, some plain scrap paper or a sketchpad, and some tracing paper.

Draw three or four simple outlines of the object you want to make and then use crayons to get different effects. Don't worry about making your design look realistic. Instead, concentrate on the mix of colors you will use and the shapes you want to show. It is often best to keep the design simple. That way, the effect you want will be easier to achieve.

Colored felt-tip pens

Eraser

Colored pencils

Stencil paper

Tracing paper

SKETCHING AND TRACING

When you are planning your work it may help if you look at references to copy or to inspire new ideas of your own. For instance, if you are fabric-painting a T-shirt you may want to find a photo or a magazine picture to copy. Trace the outline of the picture. Then cut out the traced shape and draw round it onto the fabric or the paper you are using for your craft.

ENLARGING A DESIGN

You may find a reference picture that you want to enlarge to fit your craft object. Here's how:

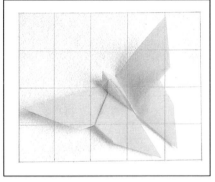

I First, draw a square grid over the picture. Use a ruler and pencil to do this, dividing it up into equal squares. If you don't want to draw directly onto the reference, tape tracing paper over it and draw your grid onto this.

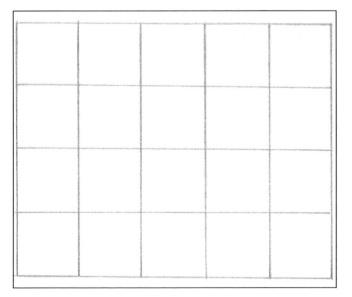

2 Decide roughly how big you want the picture to be (for instance, twice or three times as big as the original). Then, draw a larger grid on paper with the same number of squares, but that much bigger.

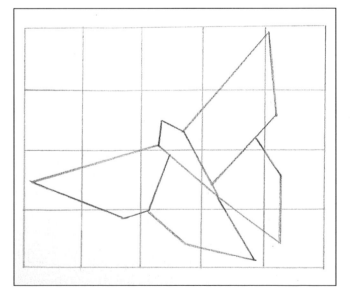

3 Using the first, smaller grid as a guide, copy the picture onto the larger grid you have made. Notice which parts of the picture fit into which square. The squares in the grid shown above are twice the size of the squares in the smaller grid.

13

Paper flowers

Paper and thin card can be cut and folded to make all kinds of clever-looking objects! Either use pre-colored paper, or paint onto it before or after you have made a model. Keep a collection of paper scraps in an envelope or folder so that you always have pieces to use. Start by practicing the basic techniques shown below.

SCORING CARD

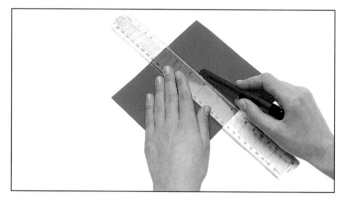

1 *To make a neat fold in thin card, it is best to "score" the foldline first by laying a ruler along the line and "drawing" along the ruler edge with the blunt edge of a pair of scissors.*

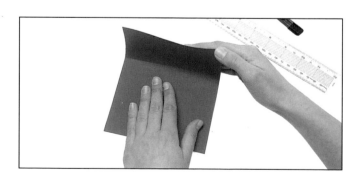

2 *Fold the foldline, bending the card the opposite way to the scored line. It will fold with a neat, sharp edge.*

PAPER FLOWERS

Use paper folding to make these pretty flowers. They will last much longer than the real thing, so they make an ideal present.

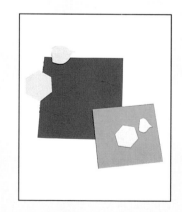

1 *Cut out a six-sided template from one piece of card and a petal shape from another piece. Place the first template in the center of a piece of colored paper and draw round it. Place the petal template against each side in turn, tracing round it each time to make a flower shape with equal-sized petals.*

2 *Make a smaller flower shape in the same way, using different-colored paper. Then, cut out both flower shapes and glue the smaller shape onto the center of the larger one.*

◄ *To make an unusual table decoration, try floating your favorite selection of paper flowers in a glass bowl filled with colored water.*

Put some paint or ink in the water to color it.

3 *Cut out a circle of paper for the center of the flower. Snip into the edge all the way around and bend the frayed edge upwards. Stick this onto the center of the flower with glue. Bend the petals upward to make the flower look more realistic.*

4 *You can make lots of flowers in this way, with different size and color petals and center. If you like, cut some leaves and glue them to the flower shapes. Make them long and spiky, or rounded and feathery.*

For stems use long, thin tubes of green card.

Cut out leaves and glue them to the inside top of the vase.

▲ *This paper vase is ideal for displaying your flowers. Make it by gluing strips of colored card around a toilet-roll tube. Then cut flaps at the top, fold and glue to the back of the flowers.*

Paper puppets

Make a mouse and some walking finger puppets decorated with folded and curled paper. Then make a little stage for them to perform on. They make good miniature presents, too.

Mouse Theatre

Put your finger in the back of this mouse to make it creep along. To curl the card for its head and body, put it under a ruler, and pull it upward in a curve.

What you need

....

Pink and white paper
Colored thread
Scissors
Ruler
Glue
Box
Colored tissue paper

Finger Mouse

1 Cut out a semicircle of pink paper and snip off one end. Cut a fringed strip of white paper with a red dot in the middle for the whiskers and nose. Cut out ears and eyes as shown.

2 Fold the semicircle around and glue it to make a cone. Glue on the whiskers, eyes, and ears, as shown. Cut out a pink rectangle, fold it round, and glue it to make a body tube. Glue it behind the mouse's head and glue a curly tail to the back.

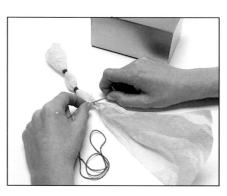

1 To transform a box into a stage, first paint it or cover it with paper. Then measure around the top and cut a slightly longer length of tissue paper. Tie thread around the paper at intervals, as shown, to make a row of tissue paper bunches. Fan out the paper a little between the threads.

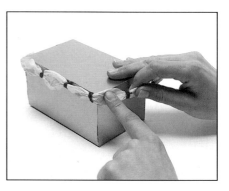

2 Use a thin paintbrush to dot glue onto the back of the pieces of thread along the tissue paper strip. Affix the strip to the outer top edge of the box for a theater stage decoration. You may need to do an edge at a time, making sure that it has stuck before going on to the next side.

Hold the glued edges of the body and head together until they feel firm. Otherwise the edges may spring apart.

Here are some more ideas for fun finger puppets. You will be able to think of many more!

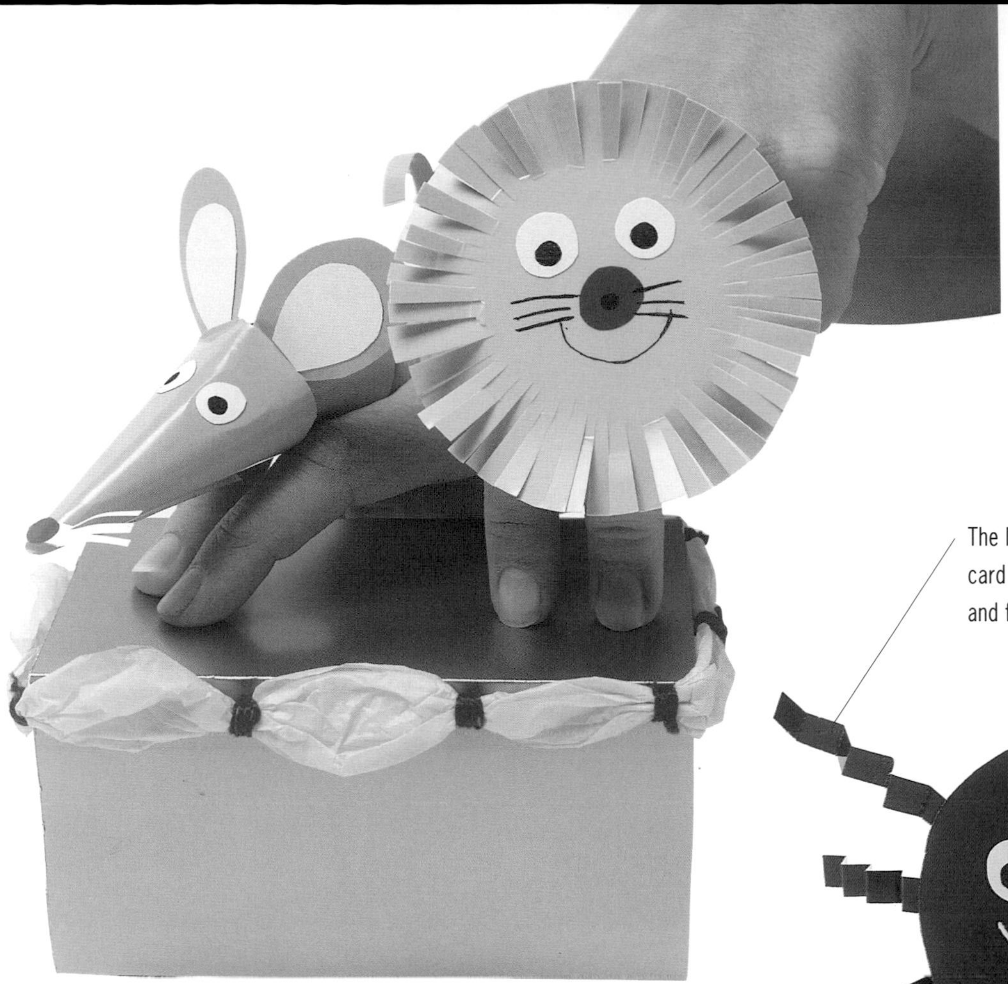

▲ *Make your finger puppets dance on top of the theater box. You could use two at a time, one on each hand.*

The lightning is made from card that has been scored and folded.

Use a black disc of card as a base for this thundercloud.

Make a head and some clothes, as shown.

A paper tube that will fit two fingers makes a puppet body.

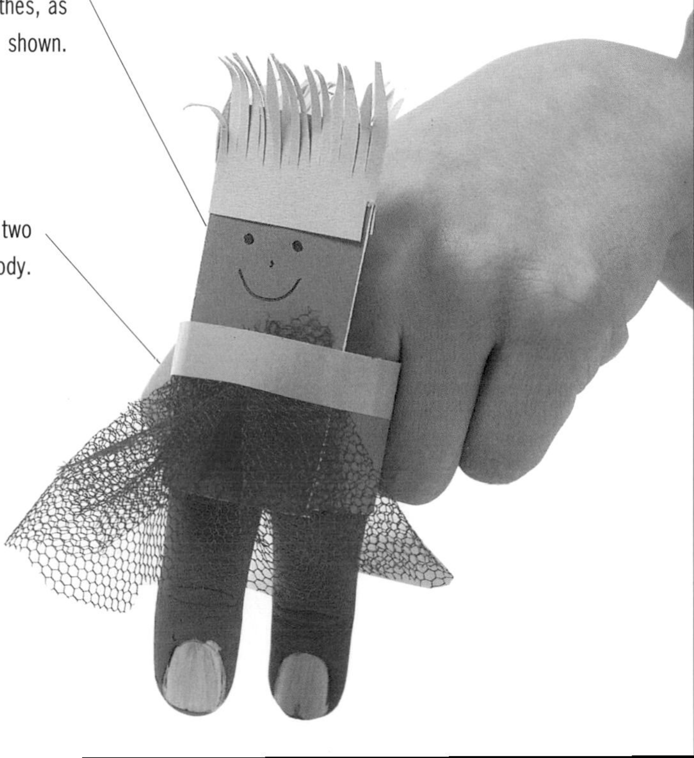

two finger holes

◄ *This funny Jack Frost is made from a disc of black card.*

17

Stenciling

STENCILING IS A QUICK WAY TO make things look as if they have been printed. By cutting out simple shapes from card and dabbing paint through the holes, you can "print" patterns repeatedly. Then you can decorate all kinds of objects, such as envelopes, writing paper, cards, paper tablecloths, and even three-dimensional objects, such as boxes.

PICTURE PATTERNS

A paper doily has pre-cut holes that make it ideal for stenciling patterns. Tape the doily on plain paper and dab different-colored paint over it.

Move the doily only when the paint is fully dry.

MAKING STENCILS TO USE ON PAPER OR CARD

Follow the steps below to stencil on paper. Cut the stencils on an old tray and then use bright paint to transfer the shapes to colored paper.

1 *Draw the shapes you want on card, spacing them out evenly for a clean, finished effect.*

2 *Cut the shapes out carefully with a craft knife. Then position the card on the paper.*

3 *Using a stubby brush or a sponge, dab thick paint through the holes. Then carefully lift the card.*

18

STENCILED STATIONERY

Here are some ideas for making stenciled stationery. You could stencil matching designs onto envelopes and writing paper to make your own personalized stationery set.

Stencil designs onto writing paper and envelopes to make a matching set.

Stencil round the edges of writing paper to make it look extra colorful.

Stencil party invitations with balloons or bows, or stencil a birthday card with the receiver's name.

Stenciling ideas

ONCE YOU HAVE PRACTICED SIMPLE STENCILS, TRY MAKING MORE complicated pictures using several different stencil shapes. The picture shown below is a "tree of life." You could glue a miniature calender at the bottom.

Try stenciling wrapping paper using a paint spray-can. You must do this outside, or in a place where it will not matter if the spray drifts onto other things.

TREE OF LIFE

Start with a piece of thick cream or white cartridge paper. Use masking-tape to hold the edges down before you start painting. This will keep the page flat.

Cut different stencil shapes out of card - a pear, apple, bird, flowers, leaves, and a branch.

SPRAY-CAN STENCILING

The paper below has been stenciled with a regular pattern of stars. This takes a long time to cut out, so you could start by trying a pattern that is simpler and more spaced out. You could try cutting out the letters of your name.

1 *Cut out a card shape that is slightly bigger than a rectangle of colored paper. Cut patterns out of the card. Then lie the card on top of the colored paper and tape round the edges.*

2 *Hold the paint spray-can away from the card and spray evenly all over. Leave the paint to dry and then peel away the card from the surface.*

Mix the different colored paints you need. Then gradually build up your picture by stenciling, in turn, the branches, then the leaves and flowers, then the apples and birds.

◀ *Cut out stencil shapes from the sides and lid of a cardboard box and line the inside with colored paper or shiny paper.*

Paint the box in
your favorite color.

▼ *Make some wrapping paper with a pattern of your favorite animal on it, using a stencil you have made. Spray paint the stenciled pattern on, wearing rubber gloves.*

You can get different
effects by spraying
lightly in patches, or by
spraying evenly all over.

Papier Mache

Papier mache means "mashed paper" in French. This craft uses layers of paper which are soaked in glue and then stuck together to make attractive, usable objects. Papier mache has been used for centuries — it is surprisingly simple to make.

BALLOON BOWL

A papier mache bowl painted in bright patterns looks stunning. Paint the inside a different color.

1 Cover your work surface with newspaper. Tape half a toilet-roll tube to the top of a blown-up balloon to hold it above the work surface. Rub petroleum jelly over the balloon. Tear newspaper strips about 1in (2cm) x 1.5in (4 cm), and dip them into the bowl of wallpaper paste.

2 Stick the gluey paper strips to the top half of the balloon, overlapping them to make a bowl-shaped layer. When you have built up five or six layers, put the balloon and bowl somewhere warm to dry. After a day or two, the papier mache will be dry and hard. Pop the balloon and gently peel it away from the inside of the bowl.

3 Trim off the rough edges of the bowl. Paint the inside and, when this is dry, the outside of the bowl. Finish with a coat of varnish.

▼ *Paint a picture on your papier mache bowl, as shown below, or dab paint onto a plain background with a clean sponge.*

Always wait for one paint layer to dry before you paint another on top of it.

BALLOON VASE

This colorful vase is made from a long balloon using the same method as for the bowl. The decorative top is made by attaching a ring of card to the top of the balloon, which is then covered with papier mache.

To display flowers inside your papier mache vase, put a glass jar inside to hold the water.

Try scrunching up the papier mache a little to create unusual shapes.

A coat of varnish will keep the dish well protected.

PAPIER MACHE DISH

Clean polystyrene trays that form the backing for meat and vegetables can be recycled as a base for making your own imaginative dishes or trays. Build up five or six layers of papier mache on the front, back, and sides. Lay it on a sheet of polythene to dry.

23

More papier mache

ONCE YOU HAVE MASTERED THE BASIC method of papier mache, you can make lots of decorative things. A mask or a funny party hat can be made using a balloon as a base, as shown on the previous pages. Since papier mache is so hard when dry, you can use it to make wall plaques as presents for your friends to hang on their bedroom walls.

PAPIER MACHE MARACAS

To make some papier mache rattling maracas, first attach a toilet-roll tube to the top of a blown-up balloon with sticky tape. Cover the balloon and toilet-roll tube with strips of papier mache, as shown on the previous pages. Leave the end of the toilet-roll tube uncovered. When the papier mache is dry, pop the balloon, and fill the inside with dry beans, such as lentils or chick peas. Now, seal the end of the toilet-roll tube with some more papier mache. When dry, paint, and varnish the maraca.

Try putting different beans in each maraca. Large beans make a low sound, while smaller beans make a high sound.

Pour the beans into the maraca through a plastic funnel, or make one from a rolled-up piece of card. Wait until the papier mache is dry first!

Keep plaque shapes simple and paint the details on the dry surface with a thin paintbrush.

Make some flowers and hang them around a window for decoration.

WALL PLAQUE

Draw an outline of a shape onto thick card (card from an empty packing box is ideal). Cut round the shape. Then build up layers of papier mache on top of it. While the papier mache is still wet, press into it with the end of a paintbrush to make lines. Mold parts of it with your fingers. When it is dry, paint and varnish it. Then, glue a loop of string to the back and hang it up on a wall.

PRESERVING PAPIER MACHE
Always let papier mache dry thoroughly before you paint and varnish it. Ideally, leave it for a few days. Otherwise it could start to go moldy under the paint.

Making boxes

IT IS EASY TO DECORATE BOXES AND MAKE THEM into extra-special gift containers. They're also ideal for hiding secrets in! Here are some simple ways to get started. Once you have tried these ideas, start designing your own personalized boxes.

SIMPLE BOX

A square or rectangular box is the easiest shape to make at first. It is easiest to wrap, too!

1 *Take the box carefully apart. You may need to ease a knife gently under any well-glued edges to help loosen them.*

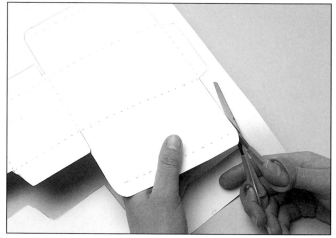

2 *Place the flat box on a piece of card and draw round the edges, using a ruler to get them straight. Cut out this shape.*

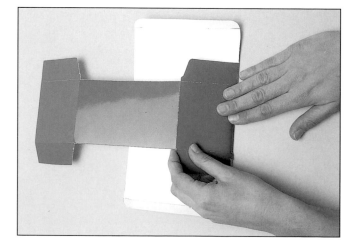

3 *Score the edges that need to fold (see page 14 for more about scoring). Fold them in the same way as the original box.*

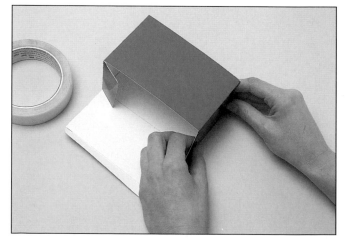

4 *Glue the edges in the same way as the original box. You may need to hold the edges together while they dry.*

Cut the flaps of the lid into teeth.

▶ *This box has been made into a monster! Glue a strip of teeth round the edge, add stand-up card eyes and a red tongue that hangs out.*

Paint your box monster a creepy color.

▼ *This box has been covered in a thick layer of glue and then decorated with rice and different colored pulses. Wait until the glue is tacky before you stick on the objects.*

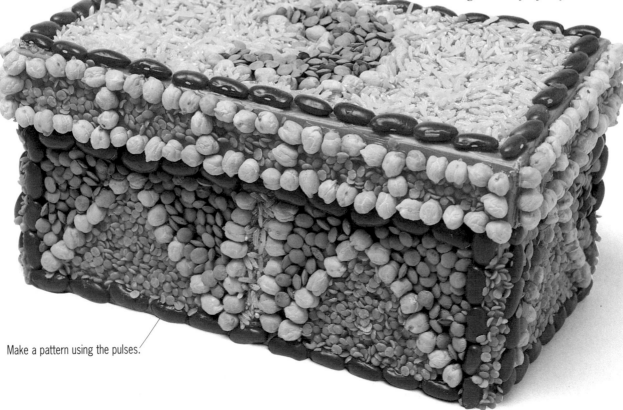

Make a pattern using the pulses.

Box tricks

HERE ARE SOME MORE FUN WAYS TO decorate a plain box. You may be able to think of some other variations of your own.

WHAT YOU NEED

Box with a lid that opens
Paints and brushes
Colored paper
Card
Glue
Scissors
Pencil

POP-UP BOX

This box opens to reveal a hidden secret — a paper jumping jack! It is attached to the inside lid and base, and unfolds when the lid opens.

Cut a strip of paper about a third longer than the box depth. Fold it back and forth into a zigzag shape. Glue a card head with a smiley face on the top.

Glue the head to the inside lid, using a paper tab. Glue the other end of the zig-zag to the bottom of the box. The jumping jack will unfold when the lid is opened!

Decorate the outside of the box with bright paints or cut-out paper shapes.

Glue paper spirals to the inside lid so that they are hidden when the box lid is closed.

Make a matching gift tag for your box.

▼ *Buy interesting shaped boxes, or save any you are given, such as unusual chocolate boxes. Redecorate them by covering them with colored paper and cut-out paper shapes.*

Fill your box with homemade sweets for a special gift!

Peek through the holes at the object partially hidden inside.

► *Cut out shapes from the sides of a box. Then line it with different-colored paper, or put something interesting or unusual inside.*

29

Decoupage

THE WORD DECOUPAGE COMES from the French word *decouper,* meaning "to cut." Cut-out printed images are glued to the surface of an object to decorate it. With decoupage you can use paper pictures to alter an ordinary household object into something unique and beautiful!

WHAT YOU NEED

Small scissors

Pictures (from magazines, birthday cards, or wrapping paper)

Empty box

Paint

Glue

Clean cloth or sponge

Varnish

GIFT BOX

Transform an ordinary box into a stunning gift box. Decorate it with colorful pictures cut from birthday cards, wrapping paper, or magazines.

1 *Paint the box all over, inside and out, with a bright color. This will be the background for the decoupage.*

2 *Cut out your chosen pictures. It is best to choose pictures with clear outlines so that you have easy edges to cut around.*

3 *Decide where to place your pictures to make an overall pattern or design. Brush glue over the back of each picture and firmly press it into position. Wipe off any extra glue with a clean cloth or sponge. Leave to dry and then varnish.*

The objects on this "fishy" box overlap to give a three-dimensional effect!

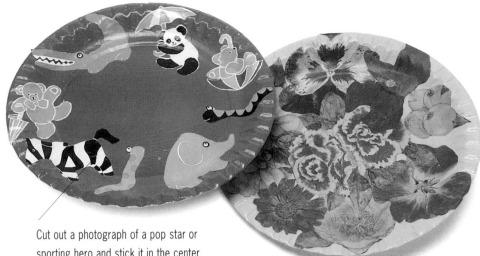

PERFECT PLATES

Find a brightly colored paper plate. Stick on cut-out pictures from wrapping paper, either in the middle or around the outside, as a border. Varnish the plate and hang it on a wall.

Cut out a photograph of a pop star or sporting hero and stick it in the center of the plate. Surround the photo with cut-outs of suitable objects.

Think about the background color carefully before you start painting.

COLORFUL BISCUIT TIN

Paint an empty biscuit tin with emulsion paint. When the paint is thoroughly dry, stick decoupage shapes or objects over it. This one has been made using pictures from old-fashioned wrapping paper on a deep red background.

When positioning the decoupage cut-outs, remember you can allow some of the background color to show through as part of the design.

◀ *This heart-shaped brooch is made from card, with a safety-pin glued or taped on the back.*

Add decoupage, matching ribbons, and lace.

Book ends

IN 18TH CENTURY FRANCE AND ITALY decoupage was used to cover all sorts of household objects, including furniture. You can do the same by making a pair of book ends from card. The ones shown here have been decorated with flowers cut out from birthday wrapping paper.

YOU WILL NEED

Two rectangles of card 14in (35.5cm)
x 7in (18cm)

Two small boxes 5in (12.5cm)
x 2.5in (6cm) x 3in (7.5cm)

Plasticine

Paint and brushes

Glue and scissors

Varnish

Decorative wrapping paper sheets

FLORAL BOOK ENDS

A pair of decoupage book ends would look great propping up your books. For extra decoration, cut out interesting shapes from the card tops, following the shapes made by the decoupage pieces.

Cover each box with decoupage.

You could cut pieces from such souces as magazines, greetings cards, or wrapping paper.

1 Measure a third of the way up the card rectangles and draw a line across each one. Score along these lines (see page 14) and bend them into an "L" shape. Paint the cards and boxes.

2 When dry, glue decoupage pieces all over them. Then put a couple of handfuls of plasticine inside each box to weigh them down and glue the boxes into the card corners.

This extra decorated card slots into the the top of the box.

▲ *If your book ends are pushed over by your books, you can make them heavier by putting more plasticine inside the boxes. Alternatively you could fill them with stones.*

DECOUPAGE SPOON

Paint a wooden spoon a bright colour. While it is drying, carefully cut out pictures and stick them in a pattern over the spoon.

Stick large bright flowers on the head, with smaller flowers on the handle.

Hang the decorated spoon in your kitchen with string.

Marbling

MARBLING PRODUCES BEAUTIFUL patterned papers, each one unique. Part of the fun is that each time you marble, the effect will be different and completely unpredictable! Although marbling is much easier than it looks, it is a messy process, so wear an apron and rubber gloves.

WHAT YOU NEED

....

Apron and rubber gloves

Oil-based paints, watered down with white spirit if they are too thick

Shallow baking tray

Thick cartridge paper, cut to fit in the baking tray

Vinegar

Newspaper

Paintbrushes

Cocktail sticks

Masking tape

MARBLING ON PAPER

1 Fill the tray almost to the brim with water. Mix in a generous splash of vinegar. If your paints are thick, water them down with white spirit to make them runny. Use a paintbrush to dribble and flick different colors onto the water surface. They should float. Swirl the colours gently round with a cocktail stick.

2 Lay the paper on the water surface, so it lies flat. Tap over it very gently with your finger to get rid of any air bubbles underneath. Air bubbles spoil the marble pattern by causing big white blobs. Leave the paper on the surface for a few moments.

3 Lift up the paper with both hands, holding onto either side. Hold it above the tray to let any excess water drain off. Then, lay the paper face-up on some newspaper and attach masking tape on either side to hold the sheet down flat while it dries.

Experiment with different color paints to get the marbled effects you want.

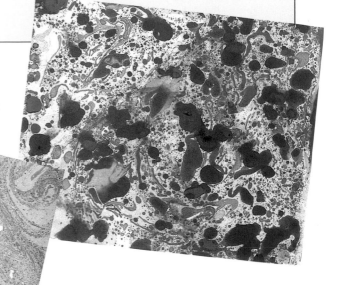

Marbled paper sheets make elegant wrapping paper. Glue a marbled fan shape to the top of the present for a finishing touch.

MAKE MARBLED JEWELRY

Save any scraps of stiff marbled paper. You can use them to make collages, decoupage (see page 30), or pretty jewelry, as shown below.

Glue marbled paper onto thin card and cut out some circles and rings. Make a small hole in the top of each one, using sharp scissors. Don't make the hole too near the edge.

Put metal jewelry loops through the holes. Thread them onto a necklace, or add earring fixings.

▲ *Make a paper party-chain from lengths of marbled paper about 7in (18cm) long and 2in (5cm) wide. Use similar sized lengths to make napkin rings.*

Earring fixing

Metal jewelry loop

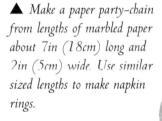

◀ *To make a frame, glue some marbled paper to card. Cut out a square from the center of the card. Glue the frame on top of a picture mounted on a card backing.*

35

Marbled book covers

TRADITIONALLY, MARBLED PAPER is used to cover books to make them look attractive and to protect them. Here is an easy way to make a loose jacket for your favorite book, and to make a matching book plate with your name on it. The book plate goes inside a book, on the first page.

WHAT YOU NEED

Rectangle of thin marbled paper large enough to wrap around the book with some to spare

Scissors

Marbled paper for the bookplate

Ruler and pencil

Glue

BOOK JACKET

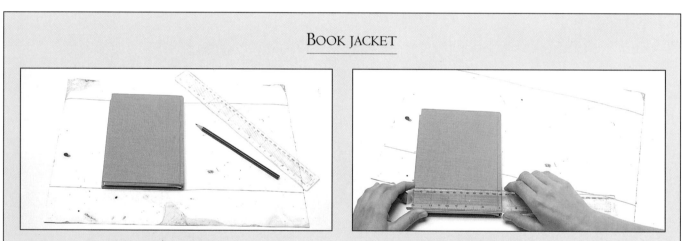

1 *Measure a book from top to bottom. Using your ruler and a pencil, mark this length on the back of the marbled paper, and trim it to fit.*

2 *Measure round the book from cover to cover, including the spine. Using your ruler and pencil, mark this width on the inside of the jacket paper, allowing an extra margin of 2in (5cm) on either side.*

3 *Trim the jacket to the right size and then fold it carefully round the book as shown. If you like, trim the inside folds to a wavy shape, or cut out a hole in the front of the jacket to show some of the book title beneath.*

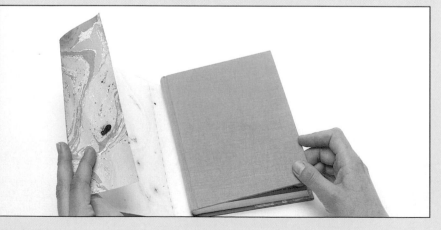

BOOK PLATE

Measure the front page of a book you want to decorate. Draw a rectangle the same size on the back of the marbled paper and cut it out. Cut a rectangle of plain white thick paper the same size.

Measure and mark a line 1in (2.5cm) all round the inside edge of the marbled rectangle. Cut round the line to make a frame and glue it on top of the plain paper rectangle.

Write on the plain paper, "This book belongs to ..." and then your name and the date. To help you to write in a straight line, draw some faint pencil lines with a ruler, then rub them out after you have written along them. Glue the book plate into your book.

▶ *Cover precious diaries, address books, and cookbooks. Not only will they look special, they will be protected by the marbled paper, too.*

Have fun experimenting with different color mixes. Try bright, contrasting mixes or subtle, pale ones.

Making books

CREATE A UNIQUE MASTERPIECE! MAKE YOUR own book, write a story inside, and illustrate it. Books come in lots of different shapes and sizes. Here are a few suggestions to try, but look in your own book collection for other ideas.

WHAT YOU NEED

....

A4 or A3 sheets of cartridge paper

Large needle

Strong thread

Masking tape

SEWN BOOK

Here is a simple way to make the inside pages of a small book.

1 *Take three or four sheets of paper (you will find it hard to sew through more than that). Fold each page carefully in half, as shown. Then, lay the pages inside each other, so that all the edges line up. To help keep them in place, you could fold some small pieces of masking tape over the edges. You can take these off later.*

2 *Thread the needle and knot one end. Sew up the middle of the book, pushing the needle through to the back and then to the front. Sew up to the top and down to the bottom; then repeat this to make the book really strong. When you have finished, knot the thread on the inside and trim the loose end.*

CONCERTINA BOOK

This concertina book has been decorated with holiday photos, painted shapes, and cut-out paper pieces. You could write a holiday diary on the other side to keep as a souvenir. To make the book, take a long piece of plain card. Measure and mark it to make three equal-sized sections. Score along the lines (see page 14).

Score one line down one side of the card and the other line down the other side, so that one section folds back and the other folds forward. Flatten the book into a squashed zigzag shape with your hand.

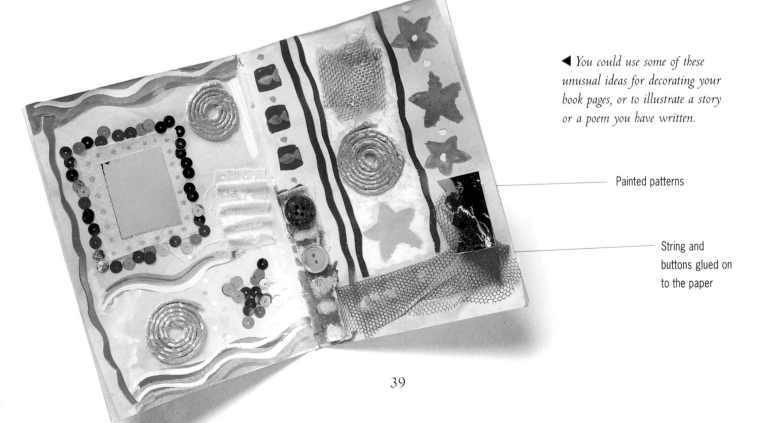

◀ *You could use some of these unusual ideas for decorating your book pages, or to illustrate a story or a poem you have written.*

Painted patterns

String and buttons glued on to the paper

Book covers

H ERE ARE SOME UNUSUAL BOOK
covers to make. Each one you do
will be a unique personal design – the
only one in the world!

WOVEN BOOK COVER

Draw a simple shape,
such as a heart, on the
cover of one of your
home-made books. Make
holes around the shape's
outline using a needle.
Then, weave colored
thread through the holes
from top to bottom.
Decorate the edges of the
book with different
colored thread, as shown.

FOLDER COVER

Decorate a project folder
cover with a picture that
shows the theme of the
project. Here, a fish
suggests a sea theme.

◄ *You could sew the pages of
your book together using
holes made with a needle and
a piece of thread. There are
many ways to do this so that
the binding is a decorative
feature of the book. It is best
not to use too many pages
though; three or four sheets a
time is usually enough.*

SPECIAL RING-BINDER COVER

If you have a ring-binder that you use for a special project, you could decorate its cover. Try gluing on pasta or dry kidney beans to give the cover a three-dimensional look.

Coat the cover of the ring-binder with glue and stick the pasta shapes on it in patterns and lines. Use dry kidney beans to decorate the spine, or try another kind of pasta shape.

When the glue is dry, put the binder on some newspaper and spray with a can of silver or gold paint. Or cover parts of the binder with masking tape to add different colored patterns.

Instead of using pasta shells, try sticking on shells for a seaside theme!

Making mobiles

A MOBILE IS A MOVING SCULPTURE where hanging objects are carefully balanced from a frame. So long as they are correctly balanced you can use almost any object – but remember to think about what they will look like when viewed from underneath and from all sides.

SPIRAL MOBILE

Try this easy mobile to start with. It is based on a spiral made from colored card.

WHAT YOU NEED

Circle of card, 6in (15cm) diameter

String, wool, or strong embroidery thread cut into four 4in (10cm) thread lengths

Plain card scraps

Paint

Brush

Scissors

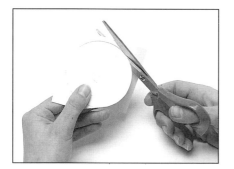

1 *Cut a spiral from the card circle and make four holes along the length. Paint and cut out four shapes of about the same size. Make a hole in the top of each one.*

2 *Push a length of thread through each hole and knot the end to secure it. Knot the other ends through the holes in the spiral. Hang the mobile up with thread.*

Hang smaller shapes from the larger ones, experimenting to get the right balance.

Hang small, light objects near the top of the thread, and large, heavy ones at the bottom.

NATURAL MOBILE

Find natural objects, such as shells and pebbles, to hang from a mobile. This mobile is made from a starfish shell, but you could get a similar effect using a coathanger.

Begin by covering a coathanger with pretty strips of material. Then, either make holes in the shells with a needle and push through the thread, or simply tie the thread around the shells. You could also use buttons and beads. Then hang everything from the coathanger.

◀ *This mobile works because the starfish shape is symmetrical, which means its shape is balanced all round. See if you can think of other symmetrical shapes you could use for the main part of a mobile!*

43

Mobile tricks

When you design a mobile, choose hanging objects that will look effective swinging in the air above your head.

SPIDER'S WEB

Making this web takes care and time, but the result is very unusual. If you want, leave out the web and hang just the spiders from the frame.

To secure the spiders, knot the middle of the thread around the frame and tie the top ends together.

WHAT YOU NEED

Three sticks, straws, or chopsticks

Ball of white nylon thread

Five small spiders (made from self-hardening clay, paint, and varnish)

1 *Lay the three sticks in a star shape and tie them tightly round the middle. Try to keep them spaced evenly as you do this by weaving the thread over and over between the sticks.*

2 *Now, weave another length of thread round the sticks, moving outwards. Knot the thread at the end. Hang the spiders from the sticks, running each thread up above the frame to hang the mobile and keep it level.*

SPACE MOBILE

This outer-space mobile glints and glitters in the light! The objects hang from a thick cardboard star shape, covered with silver foil. Don't forget to balance the objects so the mobile hangs evenly from the ceiling!

The planets are made from painted polystyrene balls – cut one ball in half to make martians!

Make a spaceship from a toilet-roll tube, covering it with silver foil, or painting it.

You could use silver thread to complete the shiny effect.

WHAT YOU NEED

Thick card

Polystyrene balls

toilet-roll tube

Glue

Silver foil

Glitter

Paint

Brush

Silver or black thread

Scissors

Tiny bells (optional)

Stars and moons can be cut out from card and painted.

◀ Your space mobile will jangle in the breeze if you can find some tiny bells to hang on it.

ADDING EXTRA SPARKLE
Dab on glue to add glitter to the space objects.

Tiny bell

Tie-dyeing

Use TIE-DYEING TO MAKE STRIPY or swirly patterns, and other exciting effects, on plain-colored T-shirts, bags, hats, and even pillowcases and sheets! You can buy small packets of dye to use. Make sure it is cold dye, which does not need hot water to make it work. Follow the dyeing instructions given by the manufacturer.

STRIPY RINGS

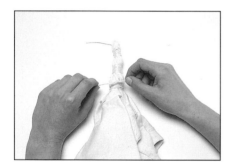

1 Lie the T-shirt flat and pull it up from the middle. Tie string round it at intervals. The dye will not reach the places covered by the string.

2 Mix the dye as directed on the packet. Use a bowl to hold the dye, and place over newspaper. Immerse the T-shirt in the dye. The longer you leave it, the darker the color will be.

3 Take the T-shirt out of the dye and put it in a sink. Rinse it in cold water, after removing the string. Then, when you have washed, dried, and ironed it, your new colorful T-shirt is ready to wear!

This T-shirt was tie-dyed using the stripy ring method.

46

PLEATING

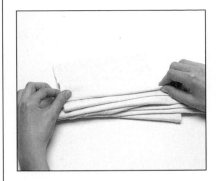 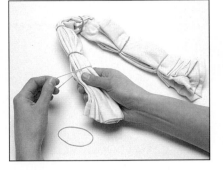 

1 Mix the dye, as instructed on the packet. Starting at the top, fold the T-shirt into pleats backwards and forwards until you get one long zigzag sausage shape.

2 Tie string or rubber bands at intervals along the sausage shape to hold it securely. Then, immerse it in the bowl of dye.

3 Leave the sausage shape for the time specified on the packet. Then, put it in a sink, snip off the string or rubber bands, and rinse until the water runs clear. Wash, dry, and iron.

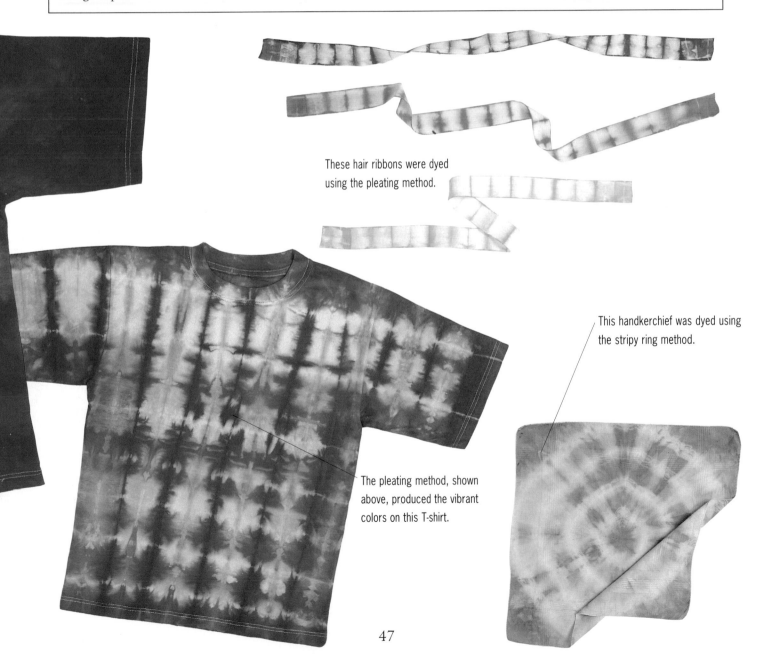

These hair ribbons were dyed using the pleating method.

This handkerchief was dyed using the stripy ring method.

The pleating method, shown above, produced the vibrant colors on this T-shirt.

Swirls and circles

Here are two more tie-dyeing patterns to try. The swirling technique creates a stunning multi-colored pattern, while stone-tying creates miniature circles with blobs in the middle. It is a good idea to practice both methods on some old rags first, before you dye a more important object. The list on the previous page shows you what equipment you need. For swirling, you also need some wide brushes.

▶ *This brightly colored T-shirt was dyed using the swirling technique.*

SWIRLING

1 *Lie your garment flat and pick it up by the middle. Twist it round into a spiral. Put two rubber bands over the spiral to keep it in place.*

2 *Separately mix four different-colored dyes into thick pastes. Then, paint a quarter of the spiral with each color.*

3 *Turn the bundle over and paint each quarter on the other side the same color as before. Put the bundle in a plastic bag, seal it with a rubber band, and leave it overnight.*

4 *Snip off the rubber bands and rinse the garment until the water runs clean. Then, wash, dry, and iron it. Now you have a stunning multi colored swirl!*

STONE-TYING

Lay a garment flat. Place a small
pebble somewhere on it and tie
it with string to keep the pebble
in place. Repeat for other
pebbles and then dye as before.

This baseball hat was tied
with string to produce
a swirly effect.

This purple pillow-case has
been stone-dyed.

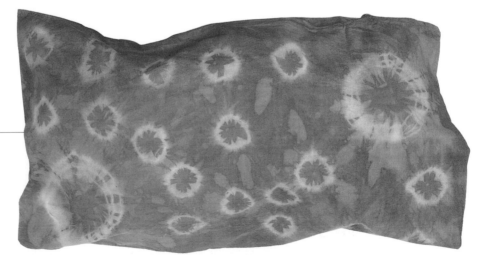

Fabric painting

Use fabric paints and pens to decorate your clothes and wear the art you have made! Use them to personalize some of the furnishings in your bedroom, too. Buy brush-on fabric paint to color large areas, and use fabric paints for writing and to add bold outlines to shapes.

1 Wash and dry the garment. While it is drying, plan what you are going to paint or draw. Sketch your designs on paper. Perhaps use a theme, such as a "holiday scene" or "my name."

CLOTHES ART

Start with a plain piece of clothing, such as a T-shirt, vest, hat, or pair of shorts, and end up with an exciting, unique piece of fashion art!

WHAT YOU NEED

Plain cotton garments

Fabric paints or pens

Paint brush

Old shirt,
to protect clothes

Newspaper,
to protect surfaces

Large plastic bag

2 Iron the garment and lie it on newspaper. If you are using a T-shirt, put a large plastic bag inside so that when you decorate the front the paint does not stain the back. When painting your design, start by painting the light colors and then move on to the dark colors.

3 Let your paint or pen drawing dry. Follow the manufacturer's instructions to fix the colors. You may need to lie a cloth over the paint and then iron over it.

You could make a special design for a friend or a relative's birthday.

Look for design inspiration from things you collect on holiday, such as this starfish.

ANNA

▼ *Shorts decorated in lively patterned rows.*

▲ *Summer hat, with the brim adorned with flowers on a green background.*

◄ *A spider's web handkerchief.*

Fabric paint projects

Here are some different ways to apply fabric paints, and some projects to try. Do not forget that you can mix fabric paints together to get new shades, just like you can with ordinary paints.

Decorating a scarf

Find a long piece of plain cotton material to make a scarf. Print on it, and add freehand painting, too, if you like.

1 *Iron your material and lay it on newspaper, or a plastic bag. Cut a potato in half and use a sharp knife to cut a shape into the surface — or if you'd rather, just leave it round. As an alternative, you could use sponges cut into shapes (you can buy these from toy shops).*

2 *Pour a little fabric paint into a shallow dish and dip the potato or sponge into it. Press the printing shape onto some scrap paper. Experiment with the method before trying it on your scarf.*

Choose a fabric paint color that will show up on the background you have chosen.

This scarf has a seam sewn around it to stop it from fraying.

52

BEDROOM BANNER

This hanging fabric banner would look great in your room.

WHAT YOU NEED

Length of plain cotton material

Pinking shears (to make a zigzag cut)

Needle and thread

Two pieces of dowelling

Colored cord

Glue, pencil, and ruler

Cut out your cotton fabric strip using pinking shears (this will stop the edges from fraying). If you want to disguise crooked edges, cut shapes into them. Lay the strip on newspaper, or a plastic bag.

Use fabric paints or pens to decorate the banner. Leave the strip to dry and follow any paint instructions for fixing colors.

Turn the banner over to the back. Use a pencil and ruler to mark a line 1.5in (4cm) from the top and bottom.

Paint a thin line of glue along the top and turn the banner edge over to make a tunnel. Do the same along the bottom line.

When the glue is dry, slip the dowelling into the seams. Tie the cord round the top dowelling to hang the banner.

Stick on sequins, or sew on beads.

If you like, stick other scraps of material, such as felt, to your banner to create a collage effect.

53

Simple batik

Batik is a method of fabric painting that is traditional in Asia. It produces brightly-colored patterns and shapes, usually with a white outline. Traditional batik is hard to do because it involves the use of hot wax. Here is an easy way to get the same effect using a mixture of flour and water.

BATIK SNAKE PICTURE

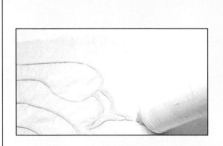

1 *Mix the flour and water to make a runny dough. Stretch out the fabric on top of a plastic bag. If you want, tape the edges down with masking tape. Unscrew the top of the washing-up bottle and pour the flour and water mix into it through a funnel.*

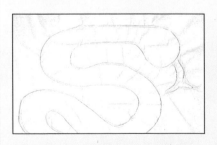

2 *Screw the top back on the bottle and paint patterns with it, or outline a shape, on the fabric. Leave the dough to dry overnight. When dry, use fabric paints to cover in the areas inbetween the dough lines.*

3 *When the paint has dried, pick off the dough with your fingers and watch your batik design emerge. You will find that the fabric under the dough has stayed white. Fix the paint colors using the manufacturer's instructions.*

◀ *Here's the finished snake picture. You could try patterns instead of a picture, or even random shapes, on your fabric. Your mistakes usually just add to the originality of your work!*

Wild designs, such as this, could enliven a cushion cover or a T-shirt.

55

Batik clothes

THE SIMPLE BATIK EFFECT WORKS WELL ON clothes. Treat it in the same way as you would ordinary fabric painting (see page 50). The bikini top shown here can double-up as a bandana. The hair scrunchy can be adapted to make hair ribbons.

HAIR SCRUNCHY

Use really bright colors to make this scrunchy stand out.

WHAT YOU NEED

Two strips of plain cotton fabric, both 1.5in (4cm) x 7in (18cm)

Length of elastic, 3.5in (9cm)

Needle and thread

Fabric paints

Prepared bottle of flour and water mix

Plastic bag

Pinking shears

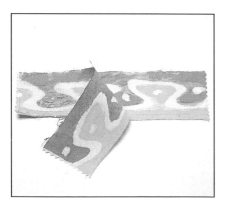

1 Make batik patterns on each fabric strip. When you have finished, iron them flat. Use pinking shears along the short edges to avoid fraying.

2 Lay the patterned sides together and put pins along either side. Sew a seam along either side.

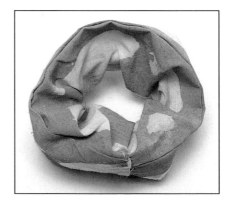

3 Turn the strip inside-out and thread the elastic through. Pull the elastic tight and knot the ends together. The fabric will scrunch up into a ball.

This bandana would look striking tied round a ponytail.

BANDANA, OR BIKINI TOP

Cut out a rectangle of fabric long enough to go round your head with some to spare. Decorate it with simple batik and cut along the edges with pinking shears to stop it fraying. Then, tie it round your chest.

▲

Batik brightens up all kinds of things — tablecloths, T-shirts, handkerchiefs. Let your imagination loose!

Starting patchwork

PATCHWORK IS A TRADITIONAL CRAFT that has been practiced for centuries. It is a good way to use up scraps of pretty material (if you enjoy it, start keeping a bag of scraps for future use). In this book, you can learn how to begin with the easiest patchwork shape – a square. If you become an expert, you could start trying other shapes.

PATCHWORK PLAN

Start by making a card template as a model for the fabric squares you make. Then plan your patchwork on graph, or squared, paper. Color in the squares the way you want and number the rows, starting at the top and going down.

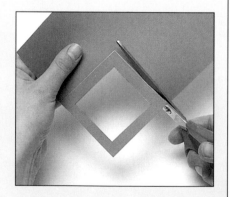

Making a patchwork plan before you start will let you see how your patchwork should look when complete.

WHAT YOU NEED

Cotton fabric pieces, 5in (12.5cm) x
5in (12.5cm), washed and ironed

Scrap card (empty cereal packets will do)

Ruler, scissors, and pencil

Crayons and squared paper, or graph paper

Water-soluble fabric pen, or dressmaker's chalk

Medium-size needle and thread

SQUARE-MAKING

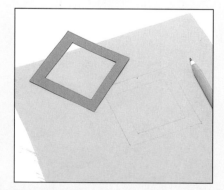

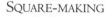

1 Draw a square 5in (12.5cm)x 5in (12.5cm) on card. Draw another square inside the first one, 0.5in (1cm) smaller all round. Accuracy is important, so measure carefully.

2 Cut out the center square, leaving a square template with a square hole in the middle. Put your template on the underside of a piece of fabric from which you intend to cut out a patchwork piece.

3 Mark carefully round the inside and outside with your water-soluble fabric pen or dressmaker's chalk. Cut round the outside square line you have made. Cut as many different fabric squares as you need.

Checkerboard patterns –
using just two colors, a
light and a dark one – look
particularly striking.

Put your different-colored fabric
squares in separate piles until you
need them.

59

Making patchwork

T HE INSTRUCTIONS BELOW ARE FOR making patchwork using handsewing. Follow the same steps on a sewing machine if you can use one. On the right, there are some suggestions for making objects out of patchwork.

Doll's quilt.

BASIC PATCHWORK

1 Start with two squares from the top row of your plan. Pin their right sides together. Knot one end of your thread and use small running stitches (a line of even-length stitches) to sew along one of the inner square lines. Oversew the same stitch twice and then cut the thread.

2 Attach the next square in the row by sewing it in the same way. Keep going until a row is done; then iron all the seams open. Make the other rows in your plan the same way. It may help to pin a label to each finished row to tell you what number it is on your paper plan.

3 Lay one row on another, right sides together with all the seams matching. Pin along the length and sew all the way along one side. Continue until you have finished your plan. Then iron the seams out flat.

DOLL'S QUILT

To make a pretty quilt for a doll, make sure your patchwork is big enough for a doll's bed. Cut a piece of plain fabric to the same size and pin it to the back of the patchwork, matching the edges. Sew along each side about 1in (2.5cm) from the edge. Then use pinking shears to trim round the quilt (this will make the edges crinkly and stops them fraying).

Easy bag

EASY BAG

Make one long piece of patchwork.
Sew some material to the back to
strengthen it if you wish (see the
doll's quilt). Use pinking shears
along either side and then fold it
in half, with the right sides
together, and sew up each side.
Turn about 0.75in (2cm) over
around the top; turn it
again, and then sew along
this edge to keep it in place.
Turn the bag rightside out and
iron it. Stitch a piece of cord inside the
bag to make a handle.

A miniature
version of the
bag without the
cord provides a
special
patchwork case.

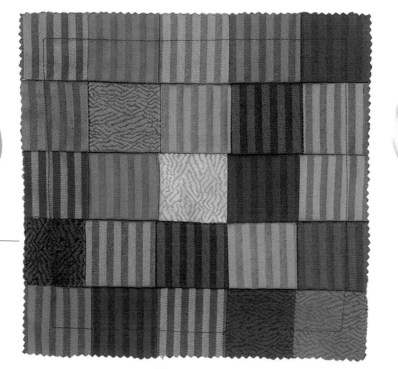

A square
version of the
doll's quilt can
be used
as a table mat.

Friendship bracelets

Y OU CAN MAKE BEAUTIFUL BRACELETS by using simple knotting techniques. It does not take long to become an expert, and it is possible to make this craft anywhere, at any time! Wear the bracelets round your wrist or knot them into your hair. Personalize them by using your favourite colors.

SETTING UP

You need different-colored embroidery threads. Knot them together with a 6in (15cm) tassel above the knot. Then secure the knot by a safety pin onto a cushion on your knee. When you become an expert, you may be able to do it with the knot pinned to the knee of your jeans!

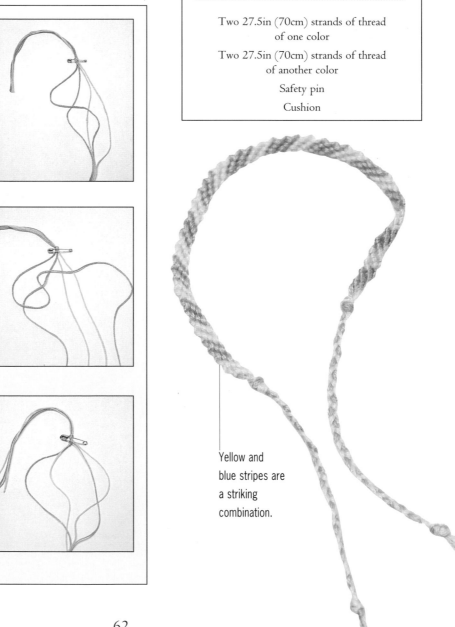

WHAT YOU NEED

Two 27.5in (70cm) strands of thread of one color

Two 27.5in (70cm) strands of thread of another color

Safety pin

Cushion

MAKING A BRACELET

1 Knot the threads together (see "setting up".) Spread them out with two same-colored threads on the left and the other two on the right. Lift the left-hand thread and bring it over the one next to it, on the right.

2 Tuck the first thread back underneath and round over the other thread again, making an S shape, as shown. Then slide the first thread up to the top and pull it to make a tight knot. Do these two steps again so you end up with two knots.

3 Move the thread on the left out of the way and repeat the first two steps using the next two threads along. Repeat for all threads. You will then have made a whole row of knots. Make more rows, starting each time with the thread lying on the left.

Yellow and blue stripes are a striking combination.

FINISHING OFF

When you get to the end of a striped section, tie all the threads in a knot. Then, unpin the bracelet from the cushion and finish the tassels by plaiting or beading them.

The easiest way to complete the tassels is to plait them together, tie them in a knot at the end and trim them near the knot. Put the two middle strands together and plait them as one thread.

If you want, plait the tassels, tie a knot, thread on a large bead and tie another knot to keep it in place. Or leave each tassel free and tie a small bead to the end of each one. Then, place your bracelet on your wrist.

You could hang friendship bracelets in your hair, as well as wearing them on your wrist.

Look for big, bright, wooden beads to use on bracelets.

PLAITING

Instead of knotting, you could do a simple plaited bracelet. Use two threads together as a plaiting strand. That way, your bracelet will be thick and bold-looking. Knot the threads as before and pin them to a cushion. Then, always working with the strand on the left, go over, under, over, under the threads to the right.

Don't tighten your knots too much or leave them too loose. You will learn what tension is best by practicing.

Try plaiting three, four, five, and even six strands. The bracelet will be thicker each time.

Macrame and more

Macrame is the art of tying knots in patterns. It is simple and quick to do, and you can make all kinds of colorful bracelets.

Try making plaited bracelets using colored string, strips of colored braid, or ribbon.

MACRAME BRACELET

This bracelet uses two different-colored sets of threads – four strands of the same color down the middle (the "filler" threads) and two pairs of threads on either side (the "worker" threads), in the second color.

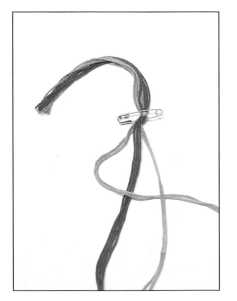

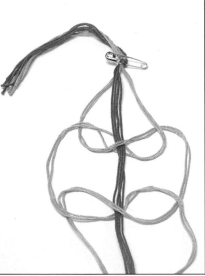

1 *Tie the threads together with a 4in (10cm) tassel and pin the knot on a cushion with the fillers in the middle and the workers either side. Use the pair of workers together, as if they were a single strand. Put the left-hand workers over the fillers and under the right-hand workers.*

2 *Put the right-hand workers under the fillers and over the left-hand workers. Then, pick up the workers which are now on the left and put them under the fillers and over the workers, which are now on the right. Put these right-hand workers up over the fillers and through the loop on the left-hand side, as shown.*

3 *Pull on both sets of workers gently, to tighten the knots you have made. Repeat the process until your bracelet is the length you want. Then, tie all the threads together in a knot and finish the bracelet tassels how you like.*

To tie a bracelet securely, use a reef knot – right end over left end and under, then left end over right end and under.

Make a plain-colored bracelet, using the method on page 62 for stripy bracelets. Then, sew beads onto the bracelet to decorate it.

◄ *Your bracelet will look bright if you use a mixture of colors that contrast well with each other. Do not forget that black and white are a stunning combination, and yellow looks great with blue, green, or red.*

Collage

COLLAGE IS THE ART OF MAKING a picture by putting together lots of different materials because of their interesting colors, shapes, or textures. You can put almost anything on a collage providing you can glue it down successfully.

Mount this miniature picture on a larger mirror tile, or a piece of different-colored card.

WHAT YOU NEED

Square of thick card 5in (12.5cm) x 5in (12.5cm) (for instance, a piece from the side of an empty packing box)
Paint and brushes
Glue, rice, and pulses

1 Paint a colorful background on your piece of card. This picture has a green background with yellow spots on.

2 Paint a thick layer of glue all over the inside of the shape. Stick pulses, beans, and rice on it to make different-colored areas. Think about using the shapes of the pulses. For instance, kidney beans make a good beak on this picture of a rooster.

3 You can add paint as well, if you like. This rooster's tail feathers are made from orange split peas, and pulses, which have been painted pink. The body is rice, painted yellow.

Make several different animals on squares of card. Then, display them next to each other.

Here's an unusual valentine, made using beans and pulses.

COLLAGE ART

Choose collage materials carefully to get the effect you want. Here are some examples of different styles to try.

Green lentils

Kidney beans

Red lentils

◀ *Stick collage pieces onto a papier mache bowl or pot. This one was covered with a thick layer of glue and then decorated with different-colored pulses.*

▼ *To brighten up a flower pot, stick buttons and beads all round it.*

▶ *If you break up an eggshell and stick it on a papier mache bowl, it cracks in an interesting way, but won't fall apart.*

▲ *This pot is covered with pieces of eggshell, spray-painted silver.*

Collage frames

HERE ARE SOME MORE WAYS TO make collage displays. The collage picture frame uses shells, but you can use anything with an interesting shape or color. The silver pictures are pulses sprayed with a can. Collage can also be used to make three-dimensional displays.

These tiles are made in a similar way to those shown on page 66, but these have been sprayed silver.

Make a hook for the back of your collage frame to hang it on your wall.

1 *Cut out a frame from a piece of strong card. Paint it a light color — this will let the collage objects placed on it really stand out. Choose some interesting things, such as shells, beads, or buttons.*

2 *Cover the frame with a thick layer of glue and position the objects. When dry, you could paint around the objects with silver paint, using a fine paintbrush. Put colored card behind the frame and display some of your favorite objects in the middle.*

Collage window

Rough out a design on paper before you start making this project. Experiment to see which colors look best overlapping each other.

What you need

Colored acetate (you can buy packs of mixed colors)

One sheet of clear acetate

Glue

Card

Poster paint or a paint spray can

Scissors

Hole punch

1 Draw a decorative frame shape on card. Cut it out and use it as a template to cut another one the same size. Cut the plain acetate the same shape as the outside of the decorative frame.

2 Paint both frames on one side. Glue the plain sides and sandwich them together with the clear acetate sheet in between. When dry, glue colored acetate shapes onto the clear acetate background.

3 Use a hole punch to make a hole in the top of the frame, well away from the edge. Loop silver thread through here and hang the frame up in a sunny window.

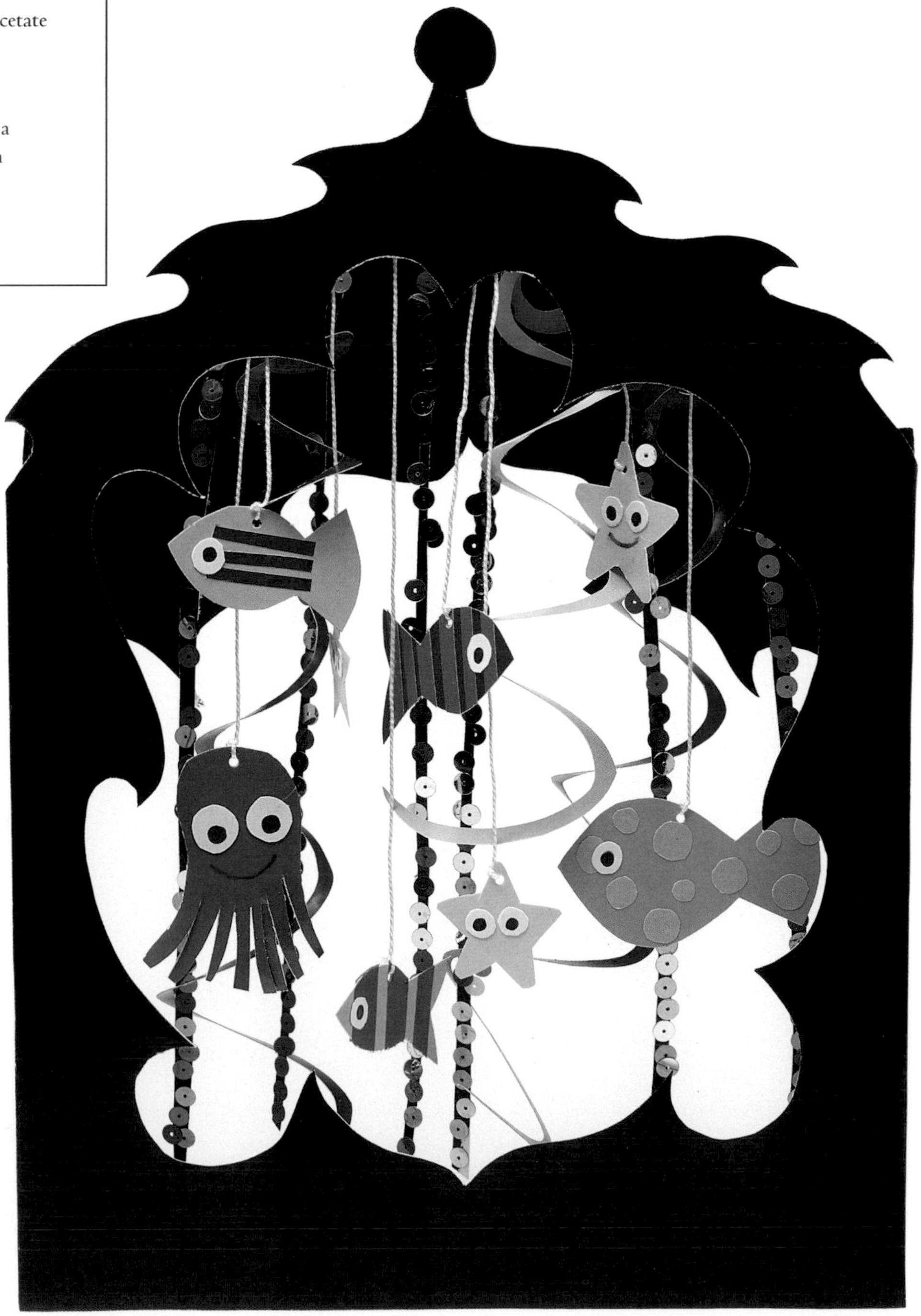

▶ *The frame looks best if it is painted a dark color. If you like, decorate it with a silver pen or stick silver foil shapes onto it.*

Toy-making

CHILDREN HAVE PLAYED WITH TOYS since ancient times and some of the oldest examples are still popular today. Using simple methods and everyday materials, you can make some of these traditional playthings.

WHAT YOU NEED

Card

Pencil

Scissors

Empty matchbox

Paint

Brush

ROCKING HORSE AND RIDER

Here is an easy way to make a working miniature rocking horse. Once you have made this one work, try other animal shapes.

◄ *The rider sits on the matchbox, her legs over the side of the horse. Try designing your own shapes using this matchbox method. You could try a boat shape, or a rocking clown!*

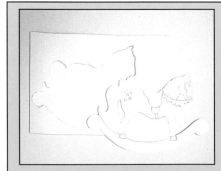

1 *Draw a rocking-horse shape on some card. Cut it out and then use it as a template to cut out another shape the same size. Lay the horse templates on a table, pointing opposite ways. Paint the side that you see.*

2 *Stick the empty matchbox (without the tray) against the middle of one plain side of the horse and then, matching up the outlines, to the middle of the other plain side. Cut out a rider through two layers of a folded piece of card, as shown.*

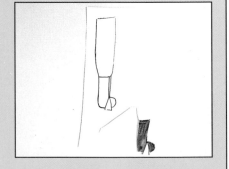

3 *Leave the top of the rider uncut at the fold. Paint it, cut out some legs from card, and then paint them. Fold each leg, as shown above, and stick them to either side of the body. Place the rider on the rocking horse.*

70

COTTON-REEL TANK

Here's a version of the traditional moving cotton reel tank.

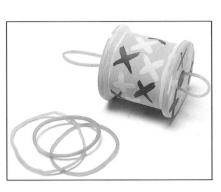

1 Pull the wick out of one of the candle tablets. Poke the rubber band through the hole in the middle (you may need to make this bigger with a sharp pencil). Make a straight groove across the top of the candle tablet.

WHAT YOU NEED

Card

Empty wooden cotton reel, painted brightly

Rubber band

Small candle (ask an adult to cut it into 0.75in (2cm) tablets for you)

Two dead matchsticks (ask an adult to cut the head off)

2 Put a matchstick through the rubber band at one end of the candle and fit the stick into the groove. Push the other side of the rubber band through the hole in the cotton reel and loop it through the other matchstick so the stick lies flat against the cotton reel. The rubber band should now be held in place by the two matchsticks.

3 Wind up the matchstick on the candle end. Then put the reel on a flat surface, let go and see what happens!

Make lots of tanks, paint them in different colors, and organize races with your friends.

Wobbling paper toys

Here is an easy way to make some toys that wobble from side to side. These ones are made from paper, but you could also use scraps of brightly-colored fabric.

What you need

Colored paper

String

Scissors

Darning needle

Cups from a cardboard egg box

Pencil

◄ *You could make other simple shapes using this method. Try a dragon or a caterpillar.*

PAPER SNAKE

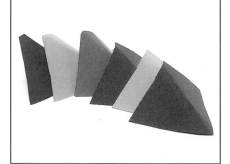

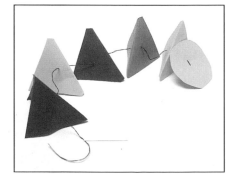

1 Draw a diamond shape on the paper. Cut it out and use it as a template to draw lots of others, and cut these out, too. You can speed up this process by cutting through more than one paper layer at the same time. Then, carefully fold each paper diamond in half.

2 Thread the needle with a piece of string about 8in (20cm) long and knot it at the bottom. Push the needle through the tips of the folded diamonds. When you have 6in (15cm) of string full of paper diamonds, thread the needle through the bottom of the card cup.

3 Paint a face on the cup. Make two more lengths and tie them onto the first one to make arms and legs. Thread on cups to make hands and feet. If you like, finish each length with a circle of card before you put the cup on.

72

Use an egg box cup for a head.

◀ *Make the body parts stiff by threading as much paper as you can on the string. Hang your doll up by a loop of thread.*

The bigger the diamonds, the fatter your doll will be.

73

Clay jewelry

FOR CENTURIES, POTTERS HAVE USED clay to create works of art. You can do the same using self-hardening clay that does not need to be fired in a kiln. You can then paint and varnish your work to make beautiful things, such as necklaces, bracelets, and badges.

IDEAL GIFTS

Jewelry is easy to make from clay. Make different shapes, such as animals and rainbows. Before the clay hardens, make holes in the shapes for earring fixings or necklace thongs. Or you could tape a safety pin to the back to make a badge.

WHAT YOU NEED
....
Self-hardening clay

Poster paint and an old tray

Metal jewelry fixings or safety pins

Necklace or string

A POINT TO REMEMBER
Use bright paints to bring the jewelry to life. Add stripes, dots and animal faces.

These badges make great gifts.

Attach your clay shapes to a necklace with jewelry hooks

74

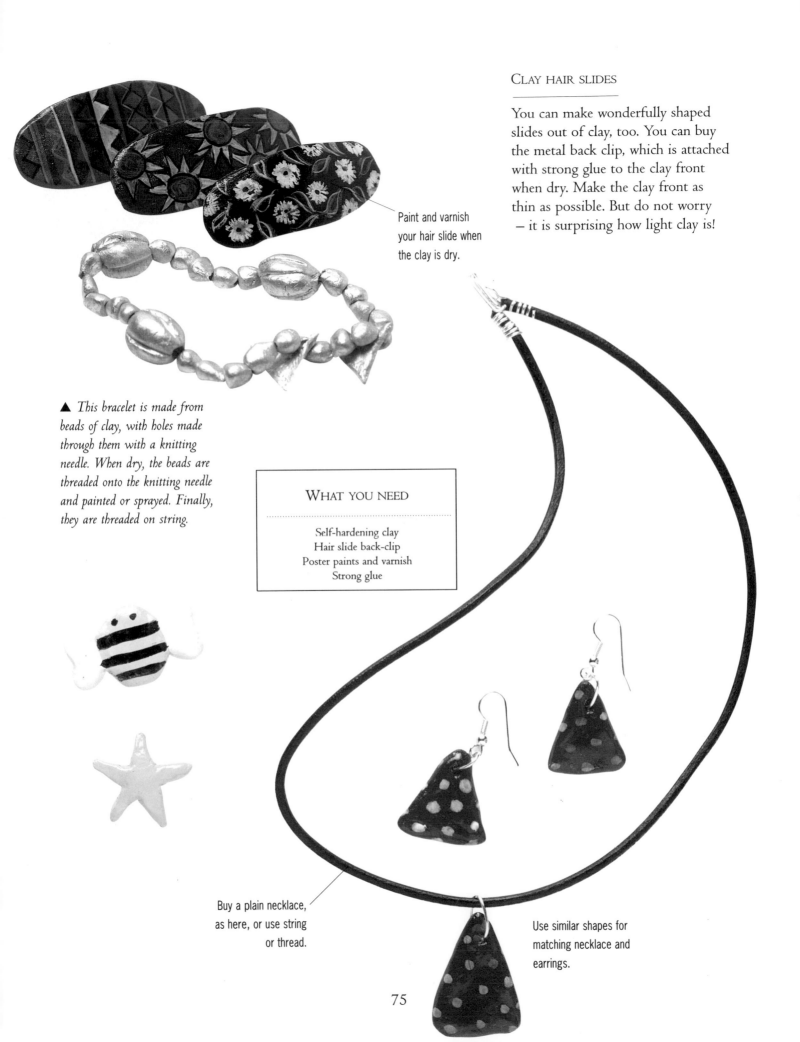

CLAY HAIR SLIDES

You can make wonderfully shaped slides out of clay, too. You can buy the metal back clip, which is attached with strong glue to the clay front when dry. Make the clay front as thin as possible. But do not worry — it is surprising how light clay is!

Paint and varnish your hair slide when the clay is dry.

▲ *This bracelet is made from beads of clay, with holes made through them with a knitting needle. When dry, the beads are threaded onto the knitting needle and painted or sprayed. Finally, they are threaded on string.*

WHAT YOU NEED

Self-hardening clay
Hair slide back-clip
Poster paints and varnish
Strong glue

Buy a plain necklace, as here, or use string or thread.

Use similar shapes for matching necklace and earrings.

Clay crafts

THE BEST SURFACE TO WORK your clay on is a wooden board. You can get different textures on the surface by using the tools listed. If the clay starts to dry out and crack while you are working on it, wet your index finger and smooth over the crack.

WHAT YOU NEED

Self-hardening clay
Candle
Poster paints
Varnish
Modeling tools

CANDLE HOLDER

Fit a candle into a spiral clay candle holder. It would look great on a dinner table.

1 Take a large ball of clay and two small balls. Roll the large ball into a long strip and wrap it round the base of the candle. Remove the candle. Make a bottom for the candle holder from another small clay disc.

2 Roll the two small balls into strips of clay. Twist them into a spiral shape. Wet the sides of the base and press the two spirals onto either side, as shown. When dry, paint the candle holder, then varnish it.

MAKING A CLAY POT

It is possible to make lots of different-shaped pots out of self-hardening clay. Paint and varnish them. Then fill them with sweets or pot-pourri to make presents. The best way to begin pot-making is to start with a coil pot. Paint and varnish it when you have finished and the clay is dry.

1 Roll out long thin lengths of clay. Wind them in a spiral to form the base of the pot and then the sides.

2 Join new lengths together with wet clay to continue the spiral up to the top. Press gently to make the pot firm.

MIRROR FRAME FROM SELF-HARDENING CLAY

Make a clay mirror frame
and decorate it with stars
and spirals, suns and moons, flowers,
or letter shapes.

▶ *Paint the frame brightly and
varnish it when the paint is dry.
Tape a wool loop to the back so you
can hang it up.*

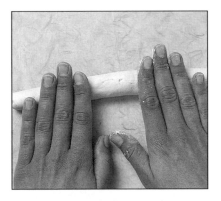

1 Put a lump of clay on a clean
surface such as a tray. Roll your
hands over it as shown until it becomes
a long evenly-shaped roll. Keep rolling it
until it is long enough to go all the way
round the edges of your mirror. It should
be quite thick all round.

2 Carefully lay the roll round the
edges of the mirror to form a
rectangular frame. Join the roll ends by
pushing them together, dabbing on some
water and smoothing over the join. Push
the roll down to fix it on and make it
look flat.

3 Use clay tools or lolly and cocktail
sticks to push different shapes and
marks into the frame. Make clay shapes
such as stars. Put small blobs of wet
clay underneath them and push them
onto the frame. Allow the finished piece
to dry and harden.

Jewelry-making

THERE ARE LOTS OF DIFFERENT ways to make jewelry. Here are some suggestions to start you off. Once started, you can look in illustrated history books to get some inspiration for your own unique designs. People have been wearing jewelry since prehistoric times, so there are lots of style ideas to choose from!

Try putting different-size beads together on a necklace.

BEAD-MAKING

Painted clay beads look attractive strung on a necklace. You could make round beads, or try other shapes, such as flowers or pieces of fruit.

WHAT YOU NEED
....
Self-hardening clay

Knitting needles, one thick, one thin.

Paint

Varnish

Paint

Plasticine

1 Roll the clay into balls and make a hole through each one with the thick knitting needle. Let them dry thoroughly.

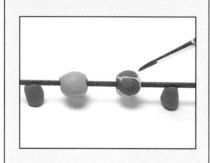

2 Thread the beads onto the thin knitting needle so that they can turn easily. Rest the needle between two lumps of plasticine on newspaper. Paint the beads a plain color.

3 When the paint is dry, decorate the beads with colorful paints. When they are dry, varnish them. Leave them overnight before you use them in jewelry.

NECKLACE

To thread a necklace, use something strong, such as plastic thread or thick embroidery thread. Either tie the two ends together or tie each thread tightly to a jewelry fixing. Before you start putting on decoration, make sure your thread is as long as you want it to be.

▶ Buy a length of beaded thread from a dressmaking shop. Cut rectangles of different colored netting. Put a few layers together and tie them in a knot around the thread. As an alternative, you could tie on short lengths of colored ribbon instead.

Fabric shops and department stores sell colored netting.

▲ Thread pasta tubes onto a knitting needle and stick it upright in a ball of plasticine. Spray the tubes with gold paint.

▲ Cut colored plastic drinking straws into equal lengths. Thread them between plastic beads or rolled-up sweet papers.

▶ Paint some corks and get an adult to pierce them with a knitting needle. Then, thread them between homemade clay beads.

Varnish the whole necklace before use.

79

Bangles, brooches, and badges

Y OU CAN MAKE ALMOST ANYTHING into a badge or a brooch, or for the decoration on a bangle.

BADGES AND BROOCHES

Start with a badge bar and glue a flat card shape onto it. Then glue objects onto the shape to make a brooch. Paint words, or glue pictures onto it to make a badge! There are some examples of this simple approach below.

WHAT YOU NEED
FOR FAN BADGE
....

Scrap card

Paper fastener

Badge bar

Tape

Glue

Photos of your family, friends, or favorite stars.

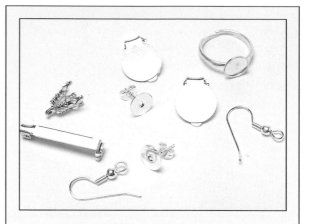

JEWELRY FINDINGS

You can buy basic jewelry parts, called "findings," in craft shops. They cost very little and make jewelry-making a lot simpler. Get some strong glue to fix pieces onto the findings. Types of finding are shown above.

▶ *Cut out four triangles. Decorate one side of each with a photo or message. Stick the badge bar to the back of one, well above the pointed tip. Lay the other triangles on top of the first one and use a pair of nail scissors to pierce a hole through all four near the tip. Put the paper fastener through this hole. Open it out and put sticky tape over the ends so they won't stick into you. Pin the badge on and then fan out the triangles.*

▶ *This badge is made from a jar screwtop. The edges act as a frame.*

◀ *This card circle is decorated with string and beads.*

BANGLES

Make a plain bangle shape by cutting a ring from a clear plastic bottle, or making a ring of card.

▼ Decorate the card shape by sticking on beads and pieces of string to get an interesting raised pattern. Then spray over it with gold or silver.

► Decorate the plastic bottle shape by winding a fabric strip round and round it. Then glue the end of the fabric where it won't show.

◄ Make several lengths of plait from thick parcel string. Make a knot at the ends of each plait so some string tassels hang down. Stick each length around a black card bangle. Line up the knots and leave the tassels hanging down.

▼ This earring is made from two paper circles. Each circle was cut from the edge to the middle, then folded back and forth to make a fan. The circles were fanned out and then glued to a card circle, which was itself glued to an earring fixing.

EARRINGS

The earring ideas shown here are glued onto a pierced ear or clip-on ear fixing.

◄ Bow wih thread sewn through the back of it. The thread hangs down. A bead has been threaded on each end.

◄ Small plastic toy.

81

Puppet-making

Puppets have been made for many centuries. There are lots of different types, some simple and some very complicated and time-consuming. The easiest ones are finger puppets and glove puppets. The most complicated are many-stringed marionettes that move like real people!

Cone puppets

Use an A6 piece of scrap paper (a quarter of an A4 sheet). Lay your finger on it and roll the paper round it, rolling slightly at an angle to get a cone shape. Tape the tip of the paper down to keep the cone shape in place. Use felt-tip pens to color the cone. You could run a pipe-cleaner through the paper behind your finger.

▶ *To perform with finger puppets, crouch behind a table and wiggle your fingers above the edge.*

A card hat gives a puppet character.

Add a paper bow-tie and tape it round your finger.

Finger puppets

These are quick, easy to make, and very simple to work – you just use your own fingers!

Tube puppets

Make a simple tube shape to fit your finger. One way to do this is to cut up the side of an empty toilet roll, cut a section out of it to make it narrower and then roll it up and tape it to fit your finger. Stick a card face on the front. For the very simplest finger puppet, just paint a face on the end of your finger and make a little paper hat, or use a thimble.

Tie a ribbon or some embroidery thread around your finger to decorate a felt-tip face.

WHAT YOU NEED
....
Scrap paper and sticky tape
Water-washable felt-tip pens

GLOVE PUPPET

The simplest glove puppet is just a paper bag with holes for your little finger and thumb! The one shown below is made from felt. You can usually buy single squares of felt in craft or dressmaking shops. Design your puppet in a sketchbook first. Then you will know what color felt to buy and what else you need to collect.

The doll's hair is a clump of wool glued to the head and tied at the ends to make bunches.

Try stitching on buttons for eyes and gluing on a mouth.

Decorate the puppet's dress with strips of lace.

WHAT YOU NEED

Two pieces of felt, both larger than your hand

Glue

Scissors

Pencil

Needle and embroidery thread

Pins

Buttons, braid, pieces of lace, etc, to decorate the puppet

Fabric pens or felt-tip pens

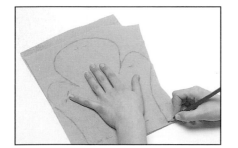

1 Lie the two pieces of felt together and pin them to hold them steady. Put your hand on the felt, with your thumb and little finger spread out. Draw a line 1.5in (4cm) outside the hand edge, running round the hand down to the straight edge of the felt. Carefully cut out both hand shapes.

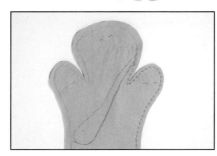

2 Put a line of pins 0.5in (1cm) inside the edge of the felt, leaving the bottom edge open. Draw a line if it helps. Sew along the line through both layers, doing plain running stitch, as shown above. Knot one end of the thread and oversew on the same spot a few times at one edge to strengthen the stitching.

3 Glue or sew on felt shapes, buttons, and wool scraps to decorate the puppet. Draw on a face with felt-tip pens or fabric pens. To make a skirt, stitch loosely along one edge of a strip of scrap fabric. Pull both ends of the thread to gather up the material to fit round the puppet. Tie the ends of the threads at the back.

Recycled Ronnie

COLLECT BITS AND PIECES FROM YOUR kitchen to make this garbageman; then work him with a stick. Try making some friends for him, and write a play for them all to perform!

MAKING RECYCLED PUPPETS

Both these puppets are made from all kinds of things – old newspaper, card, empty yoghurt pots. Use anything you can find around your home!

▶ *To perform with Ronnie, position him above a table edge. If you want, make the table look like a garbage site, with rolled-up balls of paper and foil.*

Newspaper-strip fingers

Yoghurt-pot hat, decorated with brown paper

WHAT YOU NEED

Eight empty toilet-roll tubes

Old newspaper

Glue and sticky tape

Empty yoghurt pot

Two empty matchboxes or similar-sized cartons

Empty box, such as a teabag box

Eggshells, screw tops, etc, to decorate the puppet

Old sock and string

1 *To make the head, push a ball of newspaper inside an old sock. Tie the bottom with string. Cut eyes, a nose, and a mouth from magazines, or use items, such as screwtops, to make a nose and eyes. Glue them on, with a decorated yoghurt pot for a hat.*

2 *Roll up a 2in (5cm)-tube of newspaper and pull the sock neck down through it. Tape the sock in place. Cut a hole in the top of the body box and push the newspaper tube through, with some poking out for a neck. Tape the tube inside the box.*

3 *To make arms and legs, place two toilet-roll tubes end to end, and tape them together inside one edge to make a hinge. Tape two of these tube-pairs to the bottom of the body, with the knee hinges at the front. Tape a tube-pair either side of the body to make arms.*

4 *Glue empty matchboxes onto the legs for feet. Glue some newspaper rolls to the arms for hands. Cut them with scissors to make ragged fingers. Decorate Ronnie with string, scraps of newspaper, and lettering cut out from magazines. Tape or glue a stick up Ronnie's back to make him into a puppet.*

▶ *Make a family of rubbish puppets. Write a play with recycling as the theme. Then use your puppets to perform it.*

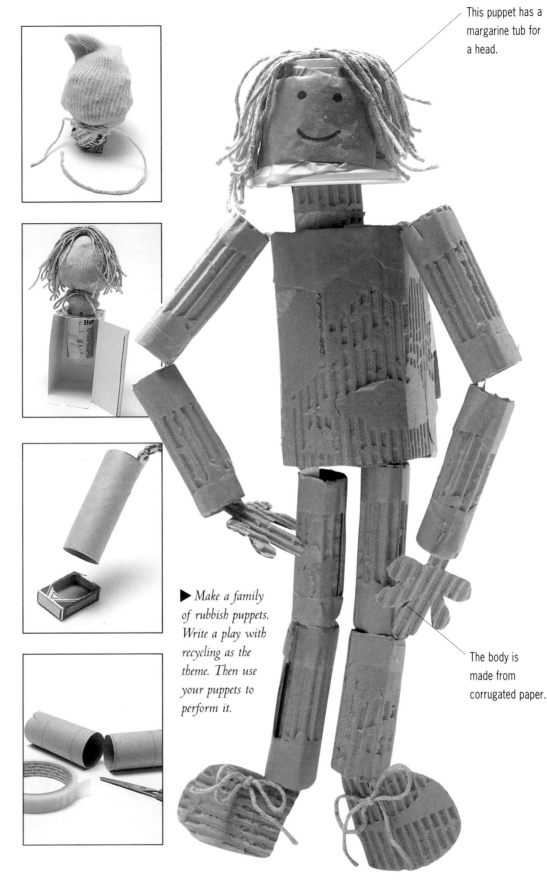

This puppet has a margarine tub for a head.

The body is made from corrugated paper.

Birthday Crafts

For a special birthday, make some personalized costumes and a card that has hidden surprises! Show you really care, too, by making a birthday gift using any of the ideas from the pages of this book.

Wheel birthday card

This card is simple to make and fun to receive.

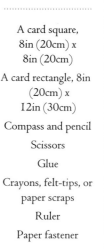

WHAT YOU NEED

....

A card square,
8in (20cm) x
8in (20cm)

A card rectangle, 8in
(20cm) x
12in (30cm)

Compass and pencil

Scissors

Glue

Crayons, felt-tips, or
paper scraps

Ruler

Paper fastener

1 *Use a ruler to find the middle of the square. Draw a circle, using a compass set at 3in (8cm). Cut out the circle.*

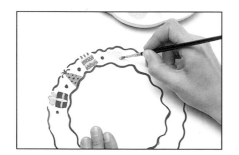

2 *Decorate the edge of the circle. Write birthday messages and draw colorful pictures on a party theme.*

3 *Make a hole through the middle of the circle, using sharp scissors.*

4 *Fold the rectangle in half, as shown. Match the edges at the top. Press down lightly on the fold with your finger.*

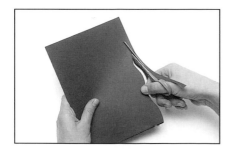

5 *Cut a wavy line along the top edge of the folded rectangle.*

6 *Decorate one side with cut-out paper shapes. Open the rectangle and run a thin line of glue along the inside edges.*

7 *Push the paper fastener through one side of the rectangle and through the circle, as shown. Glue the sides together.*

BIRTHDAY HATS

 **1** Use a compass to draw a circle with a diameter of 12in (30cm) on colored card.

 **2** Cut out the circle carefully.

 **3** Cut a line into the middle. Make a hole in the middle as shown.

 **4** Cut into a piece of crepe paper 5in (12.5cm) x 2in (5cm) to make a fringe.

 **5** Twist round the top of the fringed piece as shown.

 **6** Stick the twisted piece into the hole in the circle. Tape it in, if you like.

 **7** Fold the card round to make a cone shape that will fit your head.

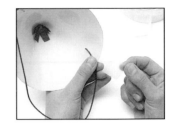 **8** Tape the cone in place. Tape on a piece of elastic to make a chin-strap.

 **9** Stick cut-out colored shapes onto the cone to decorate it.

 **10** Curl the fringe by running the strips along a scissor blade.

PARTY CHAIN

 **1** Fold some crepe paper over and under as shown above.

 **2** Draw a shape on the folded paper so it runs off each side.

 **3** Cut out the shape. Then open the paper up to get a chain.

Christmas crafts

CHRISTMAS WILL BE EXTRA-special if you make some decorations of your own. Try these easy ideas, and then flick through the pages of the book to get further inspiration. If you hold a different kind of yearly festival, adapt the Christmas theme to fit your own celebrations.

CHRISTMAS CHAINS

Here are some ideas for making unusual tree decorations.

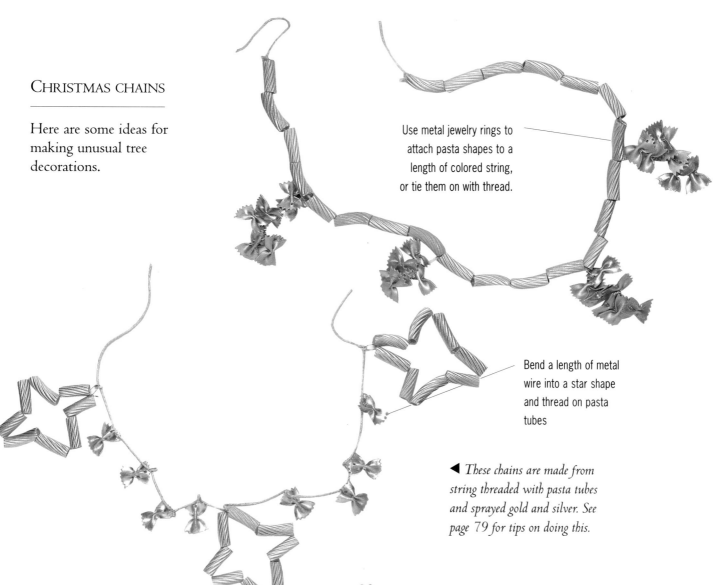

Use metal jewelry rings to attach pasta shapes to a length of colored string, or tie them on with thread.

Bend a length of metal wire into a star shape and thread on pasta tubes

◄ *These chains are made from string threaded with pasta tubes and sprayed gold and silver. See page 79 for tips on doing this.*

PRETTY PRESENTS

Use colored netting to make
impressive present bows.

WHAT YOU NEED

Netting

A needle and thread

4in (12cm) of thin ribbon, gold
thread or string folded
in half to make a loop.

Glue and foil

Scrunch some foil into a
sausage-shape and cover it
with netting to make a
decorative cracker.

HANGING MOONS

These moons are easy to
make and look great
hung in a window.

WHAT YOU NEED

A clean foil dish or
container

Scissors

Thread

*1 Flatten the foil dish, or
cut out the bottom.
Draw moon shapes on the
foil (the point of a pencil will
leave an incised mark).*

*2 Cut the shapes out of the
bottom of the dish. With
a scissor point, press gently
all round the shape of the
edge of the moon to make a
pattern, as shown.*

*3 Make patterns on both
sides of the foil using a
pencil point, as shown. Make
a hole in the top of the moon
and push through a loop of
thread to hang the mobile.*

Present-wrapping

HERE ARE SOME EASY WAYS TO WRAP and decorate presents so they look almost too good to open!

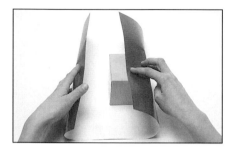

1 To cover a square-shaped box, wrap a larger piece of paper round it so that an edge hangs over either end. These edges should measure about half the length of the box. Secure the paper with sticky tape.

2 Fold both side edges into the middle in turn, creasing the paper to make them lie flat. The top and bottom edges are now triangle-shaped. Bring them together to meet in the middle, and tape them.

1 To cover an oblong-shaped box, fold the paper round it, with an edge hanging over either side. These edges should be as wide as the depth of the box. Tape the paper in place along the box.

2 Fold down a top edge so it lies flat. Then, fold in two side edges, creasing the paper so it lies flat. Fold up the bottom edge and turn over the pointed tip to make it neat. Tape it in place.

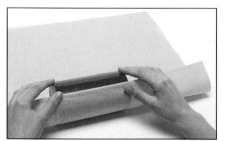

1 To wrap a present inside a pretty cracker shape, put the gift inside a cardboard tube. Wrap paper round the tube with the edges hanging over about 4.5in (12cm) at both ends.

2 Tape the paper to secure it round the tube. Then, twist the ends and tie them with ribbon, bunching up the wrapping paper. Snip the ends of the cracker into a fringe, or a zigzag line.

Crepe paper makes good wrapping paper since it is light and easy to fold.

90

These printing blocks can be used to make the colorful wrapping paper, shown below

WHAT YOU NEED

A square of card
6.5in (14cm) x 6.5in (14cm)

Two card rectangles
6.5in (14cm) x 4.5in (10cm)

Compass and pencil

Scissors

Glue

Crayons, felt-tip pens, or paper scraps
to decorate the card

Ruler

Paper fastener

PERSONALIZED PAPER

To make your own unique wrapping paper, buy some plain-colored sheets. Then, cut out some squares of card for printing blocks. Stick string on the card in shapes, such as flowers, fish or hearts. When dry, dab poster paint onto the string and press them down firmly over the wrapping paper. You will need to keep adding more paint so that each printed shape is bright and sharp.

Add two or more printed shapes to one piece of paper.

Index